DATE DUE		

AGATHA CHRISTIE

THE MURDER ON THE LINKS

ADAPTED BY FRANÇOIS RIVIÈRE

ILLUSTRATED BY MARC PISKIC

HARPER

HARPER
An imprint of HarperCollins*Publishers*
77-85 Fulham Palace Road
Hammersmith, London W6 8JB
www.harpercollins.co.uk

First published by HARPER 2007
1

Comic book edition published in France as *Le Crime du Golf*
© EP Editions 2003
Based on *The Murder on the Links* © 1923 by Agatha Christie Limited,
a Chorion Company. All rights reserved.
www.agathachristie.com

Adapted by François Rivière. Illustrated by Marc Piskic.
English edition edited by Steve Gove.

ISBN-13   978-0-00-725057-8
ISBN-10   0-00-725057-6

Printed and bound in Singapore by Imago

FRANCE. ON THE OUTSKIRTS OF AMIENS ...

These were battlefields in the war.

An army officer! How exciting! Wait 'til I tell my sister. We are both actresses, kind of travelling performers.

Mm... Yes, I know. I was wounded on the Somme. Captain Hastings at your service, Madam!

You may call me Cinderella. I think the name rather suits me.

Goodness me. *Ha!* What will my friend Poirot say when I tell him I met Cinderella?

Comœdia Illustré

LONDON, THE NEXT DAY, AT POIROT'S RESIDENCE.

You are almost on time for breakfast this morning, *mon ami.* You have recovered from the Channel crossing?

Well, I certainly wasn't seasick on such a short journey! Have you read your post?

There is nothing of interest. Only bills ... The great criminals, they no longer exist. See for yourself, *mon ami.*

"We would be most grateful if you would come and give a talk on the art of detection to a Boy Scout troop in Reading ..."

And this one? A letter from Jack the Ripper issuing me a challenge, perhaps?

No, Poirot. Here is something distinctly out of the ordinary. It has *"Come quick!"* scrawled at the bottom.

A Mr Renauld of Merlinville-sur-Mer asks you to come urgently to France. He fears for his life and is willing to pay whatever you desire. He adds that you may need to go to Santiago. That's in Chile!

There is no time to lose. Will you accompany me? Across the Channel once more, Hastings!

I am wondering, *mon bon ami*, if this Monsieur Renauld could be the South American millionaire of that name. But I am concerned by his postscript.

"*Come quick!*"? Probably a way of making sure you'd come. You know, I thought I'd heard his name before ...

No one to meet us! This makes me uneasy — Renauld wrote that he would send a car. Can you find a taxi, Hastings?

Villa Geneviève, please, driver.

I'm sorry, sir, I don't know where that is.

MERLINVILLE sur

Then we must look for it, *mon ami*.

Villa Geneviève, mademoiselle?

It's a little further down the road, hidden behind the trees.

Mon Dieu, Hastings, the police! We are too late ...

Monsieur Poirot! My friend, your arrival is most opportune.

Inspector Bex! What brings you here?

Monsieur Renauld was murdered this morning.

But it was he who asked Poirot to come!

He foresaw his own murder? That upsets our theories considerably!

When was the murder committed?

The body was discovered early this morning.

Poirot, allow me to introduce Monsieur Hautet, the examining magistrate in charge of the case ... and Dr Durand, who can confirm the time of death.

I believe my friend, Hercule Poirot, has something of importance to show you.

Indeed, Monsieur Hautet. I have a letter from the deceased, which may be of assistance to you.

We are indebted to you, Monsieur Poirot. I hope you will honour us by assisting our investigations.

Mon Dieu! Madame!

What on earth ...?!

Madame Renauld was freed at once by the maid, Françoise Arrichet. Would you like to speak to her?

Indeed I would, Inspector!

Tell me, did you notice anything unusual last evening?

Er ... no. Madame went to bed early. Monsieur sent the chauffeur home and was in his study as usual until ... er ...'

Please continue. Then what happened?

Er ... I let the lady in, like I do every evening ...

Which lady?

Madame Daubreuil. She's a friend of Monsieur. She lives at Villa Marguerite, down the road.

Well, this is a surprise! So Monsieur Renauld and Madame Daubreuil were ... ahem! Are you sure there can be no doubt about it?

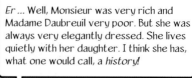

Er ... Well, Monsieur was very rich and Madame Daubreuil very poor. But she was always very elegantly dressed. She lives quietly with her daughter. I think she has, what one would call, a *history!*

Indeed? And what did Madame Renauld have to say about this — friendship?

I don't think she suspected anything ... at least not in the beginning. But then she started to suffer, to grow pale. But it's not surprising when such things are going on. No reticence, no discretion!

What time did Monsieur Renauld go up to bed?

He came up ten minutes after me. I heard nothing after that. In my opinion, Monsieur, the Mafia were on his track!

Thank you, *ma fille.* You may go.

Monsieur Poirot, this is Ernest, Monsieur Renauld's valet ...

Thank you, *mon ami.* Ernest, did you let in Madame Daubreuil last evening?

Madame Daubreuil? No, she didn't come. A lady came here, but it was someone else.

Had you seen her before, Ernest?

No, Monsieur. But she spoke English ...

... and I heard Monsieur say to her as he opened the door, "Yeas, yeas— but for Gaud's saike go naww!"

Well, gentlemen, what are we to make of these two contradictory witnesses?

It was Ernest who let in the visitor. And clearly Françoise dislikes Madame Daubreuil.

A good point, Monsieur Bex. But I was forgetting ... we haven't yet told Monsieur Poirot there was yet another woman in Renauld's life!

This letter, Monsieur Poirot, was found in the dead man's pocket.

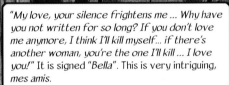

"My love, your silence frightens me ... Why have you not written for so long? If you don't love me anymore, I think I'll kill myself... if there's another woman, you're the one I'll kill ... I love you!" It is signed "Bella". This is very intriguing, mes amis.

Renauld was involved with this English woman. He comes here, meets Madame Daubreuil and starts an affair with her. A jealous woman such as Bella could have stabbed him, but how could she have moved the body and dug the grave?

You're right. The murder was committed by a man.

The letter you received from Monsieur complicates matters ...

Renauld was a man of the world. He would not be likely to call upon a detective to protect him from a lovesick woman!

I'm sure the answer lies in Santiago. I'll cable the city's police at once!

Excellent.

The body is in here. We brought it here after removing it from the grave dug by the murderer.

Bien, let us take a look.

One can see by his face that he was stabbed in the back. With what weapon was the crime committed?

A pretty little tool for a murder!

Alas, we found no trace of fingerprints.

I see Monsieur Renauld wore only underclothes beneath the raincoat ...

Indeed, it was a curiously long overcoat ...

Madame Renauld will see you. Please try not to distress her.

Mon ami, you should be aware that this is not the way of Hercule Poirot!

Thank you for coming, Monsieur Poirot. Please sit down, gentlemen ...

Please tell us all you can, madame ...

I woke up with one attacker's hand on my mouth.

The other man was threatening my husband with my paper-knife. Then they forced him to get up and accompany them into the bathroom.

Did they speak to one another?

Yes. It sounded to me like Spanish, the kind spoken in South America. One of them asked my husband, "The secret! Where is it?" And the other added, "Where are your keys?"

Françoise told me that the safe had been forced open. Then those two villains made my husband go with them. But he had time to tell me he would be back before dawn. Poor man!

Your husband sent me a letter claiming he was in danger. Do you know anything of this?

?

What's this? Look at this watch. It says seven o'clock. But the time is only five.

No. But certainly he had many enemies.

That's strange, it's working perfectly well.

Indeed so, although it appears it was damaged during the assault ...

Possibly the watch gains, is that so, madame?

Yes it gains a little. But not that much.

Madame, do you know of a woman named Bella? And are you aware that your husband received a visitor last evening?

No! What are you suggesting?

But that's my little dagger!

It's also the murder weapon!

You must now be very courageous, madame. If you feel up to it, we must ask you to undertake the painful task of identifying your husband's body.

Paul ... my poor dear Paul!

Never before have I heard such love and grief in a woman's voice. My little idea was all wrong. *Eh bien!* I must start again!

THE NEXT MORNING ...

It is strange to me that the servants heard nothing, Hastings.

But it was the middle of the night. Everyone was asleep.

Hm ... I would expect that the attackers would force open the window.

That is the bedroom where we were, is it not? It would be easy to reach it!

Yes but there would be footprints in the flowerbeds.

What are you doing, Poirot?

Here are plenty of footprints for you, Inspector Bex!

No doubt they belong to the gardener.

So you think them of no importance? I do not agree with you!

I have a little idea that these footprints are the most important things we have seen yet.

I too have something to show you. Shall we proceed, gentlemen?

I know all about the case, Monsieur Bex, and I think this is where we'll find a clue. I see your men have been trampling all over the footprints!

They were made by the workmen ...

This is where the assailants came through the hedge. The footprints in the middle belong to Monsieur Renauld.

The physical clue. That is what you seek, *eh*?

Of course.

One of the assailants wore these gloves. They probably belong to Renauld's gardener. And the grave was dug with a spade from the house.

And does this lead pipe also belong to the murdered man?

That's of no interest to me.

Perhaps, it should be, *mon ami.*

It was a strange place, Monsieur Giraud, to choose to bury the body. The workmen could hardly miss it.

Exactly. That confirms that the murderers must be foreign. They weren't aware that work on the golf course had not yet been completed.

Well reasoned ...

If you say so, mon ami ...

Unless they *wanted* the body to be discovered!

Mon cher Hastings, you have just seen at work a human foxhound.

Well at least he's *doing* something.

He is? And what about that piece of lead pipe? Let Giraud carry on with his search ... *I'm* going to use my little grey cells!

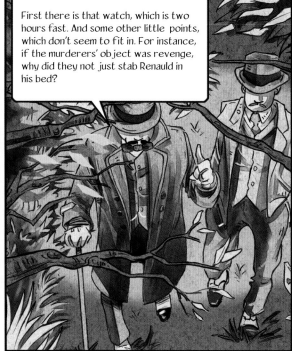

First there is that watch, which is two hours fast. And some other little points, which don't seem to fit in. For instance, if the murderers' object was revenge, why did they not just stab Renauld in his bed?

Because they wanted to know "the secret", Poirot.

14

Tell me, my good fellow, how long have you been working here?

For twenty-five years, monsieur.

These geraniums are magnificent. Have they been planted long?

Yes, some time ago. But they have to be replaced regularly.

Ah, and you planted some just yesterday, did you not?

Monsieur has a sharp eye.

They are truly splendid. Might I have a cutting?

But certainly, monsieur.

Ah, Poirot, now I see! How clever of you!

At last I am on the right track! But Hastings, I am sure Giraud will take not the least interest in these footprints.

This is Madame Daubreuil's villa. Apparently more than 200,000 francs have been recently deposited in her bank account.

Presumably courtesy of Monsieur Renauld ...

She is a mysterious woman. Nothing is known of her past life ...

And what of her daughter?

Such a beautiful young girl must wonder about her mother's mysterious past. Let's see if we can discover a little more of it!

We are sorry to disturb you, mademoiselle. Will it be possible to speak with your mother?

I shall fetch her. Please come in.

What is it you want, gentlemen?

We have come to ask whether you can throw any light on the circumstances of Monsieur Renauld's death, madame.

You have no right to ask me such questions! It's utterly improper.

Madame, we are investigating a murder! Did Monsieur Renauld confide in you that he was in danger? Did he ever mention Santiago?

Never! Can his wife not tell you such things?

Sometimes a man confides in his mistress rather than his wife.

Monsieur Hautet, you insult me. Kindly leave my house!

The French police are a marvel, Hastings. The information they possess about everyone's life is extraordinary.

Monsieur Poirot!

It's Mademoiselle Daubreuil! She must have something to tell us.

I beg your pardon, Monsieur Poirot. But is it true that Monsieur Renauld called in a detective before he died — and that you are he?

It is quite true, mademoiselle.

What is it you wish to know, mademoiselle?

Is anyone ... suspected?

Suspicion is in the air, mademoiselle.

I shall let you into a secret. Suspicion at present has fallen on two Chileans from Santiago.

Oh! — look at the time! I must return home. *Maman* will have missed me.

You are clearly quite taken by that young girl, Hastings.

She is very pretty ...

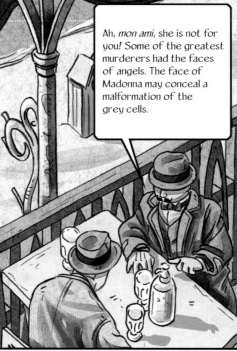

Ah, *mon ami*, she is not for you! Some of the greatest murderers had the faces of angels. The face of Madonna may conceal a malformation of the grey cells.

Myself, I am wondering why her mother's face seems so familiar to me. I rather fancy it was in connection with a murder!

This way, *mon ami*. How is Madame Renauld?

She is still terribly upset.

Ah! True unto death ... and beyond! However, surely your mistress would have been justified not to grieve ...?

Madame never offered Monsieur Renauld a word of protest. Even though he was often far from kind to her and had a fierce temper.

The day he quarrelled with his son, Jack, the whole market heard!.

Indeed! And when did this occur?

It was the day Jack left for Paris. Monsieur was angry all that day after their argument. But I don't know what they argued about.

I see. Thank you for the information, monsieur.

Poirot, if you'll allow me, I'd rather like to see what Giraud's up to.

Ah, the human foxhound! Not at all, *mon ami*. Go ahead!

You?!

You too! What a surprise!

Cinderella, if I'm not mistaken!

So you remembered my name ...

Of course. But aren't you going to tell me the real one now, you little mystery? Or why you're here?

Oh, *that!* I suppose you've heard of members of my profession "resting"?

At *chic* and expensive watering-places?

Not quite so expensive if you know where to go ...

And what are you doing in Merlinville? Surely you're not in on the crime at the Villa Geneviève?

Yes ... In fact I'm here with my friend Hercule Poirot, the great detective.

How thrilling! I'd love to see where the wicked deed took place.

But look here, miss ... that's impossible.

Oh, come on, do show me ...

So the poor man's body is in here?

Er ... yes, indeed.

And ... that dagger there in the glass jar?

That's the murder weapon.

Oh, it's too much ... I don't feel very well ... Water, quick! I need water ...

Come, sit down ... You should never have asked me ...

21

Ah! There you are at last, *mon ami*.

Hm, I'm sorry Poirot, but ...

Stop, stop, stop ... Don't say anything! Giraud has vital information on the gardener's boots. He takes them off before going to sleep!!!

And he has made another very important discovery. A cigarette stub and a matchstick, which Giraud says are commonly found in South America!

Really! And what do *you* think?

Very little. I am more interested in who let the murderers into the house and afterwards deliberately left the door open. Any theory which does not take that detail into account will prove worthless.

Ah, Monsieur Giraud, just in time! Tell me, does something strike you as familiar about this case?

A strange question! The seaside air clearly doesn't appear to suit you, sir! In any case, Monsieur Renauld's secretary has arrived.

This is Monsieur Hercule Poirot ... and his friend, Captain Hastings.

Ah, Monsieur Poirot, the famous detective! I gather that Monsieur Renauld sent for your assistance?

Did you not know that, Monsieur Stonor?

No, but it doesn't surprise me a bit.

How long were you Renauld's secretary?

Since he returned from South America, about two years ago. A mutual friend recommended me.

Did he mention any incidents in Santiago? Or any secret relating to his time there?

No, but Monsieur Renauld never said a word about his life. All I knew was that he was French-Canadian.

Did Monsieur Renauld ever mention the name *Duveen*?

Er, no ... and yet it seems familiar.

What about a woman named *Bella*?

Bella? Duveen? Are you suggesting he had a mistress? I'll bet my bottom dollar you're wrong about that!

And yet we have a love letter from Bella to the deceased ... who was carrying on an intrigue at the time of his death with a certain Madame Daubreuil ...

You're barking up the wrong tree! Blackmail, that's what it was! Four thousand pounds in two months she extorted from him. Madame Daubreuil had the screws on him all right!

Were you aware that Monsieur Renauld made a new will just two weeks ago, leaving everything to his wife?

No. He drew one up a year and a half ago, in which his wife and son inherited equally.

Madame Renauld! Are you ...?

It's all right, Stonor, I'm better now. But look who's just arrived.

Monsieur Jack!

We thought you were sailing for Argentina.

The ship was delayed. I saw the news of my father's death in the newspaper.

These gentlemen are convinced that your father's past held some mystery.

Precisely. And is it not in connection with this mystery that you were sailing to Argentina?

I was going at my father's request. He said it was a very important matter.

Did your father have enemies in Santiago?

None to my knowledge. I am convinced my mission was connected with business interests.

Can you confirm that you had a violent quarrel with your father before you left? A quarrel during which, according to witnesses, you wished him dead?

That may be so.

But I decline to state what the quarrel was about!

Eh bien. I, Hercule Poirot, will inform you, Monsieur Giraud.

The subject of the quarrel was Mademoiselle Marthe Daubreuil.

I'll grant you that's true. I love Mademoiselle Daubreuil and I wish to marry her. When I told my father, he flew into a rage. I lost my temper too ...

You were aware of this — attachment, madame?

I feared it. I should prefer Jack to marry an English girl, or at least a French girl whose mother had a better reputation!

Monsieur Renauld, why did your father object?

He spoke of a shameful mystery surrounding Marthe and her mother. But he refused to discuss the matter further. Finally he reminded me he could take away my allowance at any time.

I left in a fury, in danger of missing my train to Paris. I wrote to Marthe, and her reply reassured me. She was certain my father would give way and let us get married in the end ...

Very well. Now we must show you the murder weapon. I fear it may distress you, monsieur. I understand the paper-knife was a present from you to your mother?

Monsieur le juge! The dagger — it is gone!

25

LATER ON ...

I am glad I was not in your shoes when you had to confess to those gentlemen!

That I had been taken in by a beautiful creature who insisted on seeing the murder weapon? Yes, that was embarrassing. But it was my own fault.

No matter, Hastings. Maybe some good has come of it. In taking advantage of the situation, the murderer blundered!

Please accompany me to my room, *mon ami*. There is something I must tell you. But wait one little moment ...

Ah, I see.

Whose coat is this?

What distracts you now, Hastings? Some young beauty?

Be serious, Poirot! I was just considering that Madame Renauld is the only person to benefit from her husband's death.

Indeed so. I too have suspected her from the very beginning. As you know, I examined her wrists. She was certainly tied up tightly. Perhaps she had an accomplice?

Poirot, don't be so mysterious. What is it you really think, for goodness' sake?

I will explain, *mon ami*. But not a word to Giraud, *eh*?

26

Everyone agrees that the crime was committed at two in the morning. Madame Renauld says she heard the clock strike while the men were in the room. But I, Hercule Poirot, say that it is untrue.

The last train leaves Merlinville at seventeen minutes past midnight, furnishing a perfect alibi. And the watch was damaged so as to appear that it stopped when the crime took place. But it did not stop ...

Then we must inquire at the station. They cannot fail to have noticed two foreigners take that train!

Tut! Tut! Surely you do not believe that rigmarole of the masked men! You heard me say to Giraud, did you not, that the details of this case seemed familiar? I believe the murderer is dragging a red herring across our tracks!

Madame Renauld was not the murderess, although she was certainly lying. She said the murderers left through the window ...

But there were no footprints!

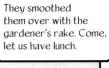

They smoothed them over with the gardener's rake. Come, let us have lunch.

I so enjoy hearing of your little romantic adventures, *mon ami*. Do you propose setting up a harem?

You do go on, Poirot! I don't in the least bit intend to see Miss Cinderella again ...

You told me she stays at the Hotel d'Angleterre, did you not?

No, the Hotel du Phare. But ...

That was an excellent meal. But now I shall leave you, *mon ami.* I must go by train to Paris.

What?!

I shall return tomorrow. Keep an eye on Monsieur Giraud! And cultivate the company of Monsieur Jack. I should like to know what kind of couple he and Marthe Daubreuil make.

What do you mean by that, Poirot?

We shall see ... And please, do not accompany me to the station. You must pay a visit to your Mademoiselle Cinderella.

HO EL HARE

A young, dark-haired Englishwoman? There is no such lady staying here. *Hm,* a short gentleman with a round head and stiff moustache has asked me the same question ...

Poirot!

28

What are you doing, Giraud?

Exactly what you were doing, Monsieur Hastings. What have you done with your Belgian fossil?

Monsieur Poirot has gone to Paris.

A good thing too! The longer he stays there, the better.

LATE THAT AFTERNOON ...

29

THE NEXT MORNING ...

Hello! Who is it?

Monsieur Hastings? I was told to inform you that another crime has been committed at Villa Geneviève!

Oh, Monsieur Hastings! It's another murder!

Who is the victim?

I don't know, monsieur. A stranger. Stabbed in the heart not far from where they found Monsieur.

Ah! Monsieur Hastings. I'm expecting the doctor any minute. But as far as I can tell, the man has been dead for at least twelve hours.

When was it you last saw that dagger?

About ten o'clock yesterday morning. Surely you don't think he was killed right here?

A fine detective you are! Did I suggest he was murdered in this greenhouse?

30

There has been another murder. We must go to Villa Geneviève at once!

Another murder? *Ah*, then I have everything wrong. Giraud will mock me, and with reason.

You'll never believe it. That devil Giraud has taken matters into his own hands. I was there when Madame Renauld and Madame Daubreuil saw the body. Neither of them recognized him.

But the doctor said something extraordinary — that the man had been dead for at least forty-eight hours.

Mon Dieu! Listen to me, Hastings. The victim was found near where Monsieur Renauld's body was discovered. And — *hmm* — he was stabbed in the chest.

Poirot, you're pulling my leg! How did you know ...

The little grey cells, *mon ami!* Now follow me. We shall take a short cut across the golf course.

The dagger was still in the wound, you say? You are sure it was the same one?

Yes, I'm certain!

Perhaps Jack Renauld had two identical paper-knives made ...

That seems rather unlikely!

31

It is a strange wound, this. There is almost no blood.

Dr Durand, do you not think the man could have been stabbed *after* he was dead?

But Monsieur Poirot ...?

And Monsieur Giraud agrees with me, do you not, monsieur?

Er ... Yes, certainly I agree.

What are you saying Poirot? That is impossible. It's absurd!

And I will add that, according to my examination, the man was not killed. Rather he died. Died of an epileptic fit!

Monsieur Poirot, I am inclined to believe you are correct.

Impossible! How can you say such a thing?

You recognize this person, Hastings?

It's Madame Daubreuil!

You are mistaken! Do you remember the Beroldy case? This, *mon ami*, is Madame Beroldy.

Madame Beroldy ... the beautiful young wife of a wine merchant, accused of persuading her lover to murder her husband so she could marry the American millionaire who adored her. His name was ... Georges Conneau?

Quite correct! Moved by her tears and her charm, the jury acquitted Madame Beroldy, and she left Paris with her small child and ...

And you believe the same scenario was repeated here, and Madame Daubreuil — or Beroldy — murdered Monsieur Renauld?!

No, *mon ami*, the case is more complicated. Madame Beroldy was acquitted. In law, she is innocent. Nor is there any evidence that she was Renauld's murderer.

But you were saying ...

Besides, why would Madame Daubreuil murder Monsieur Renauld? She does not benefit from his death. Let me remind you that Madame Beroldy had an American millionaire waiting to step into her husband's shoes.

I should like to pay Mademoiselle Daubreuil a visit. Will you accompany me, Hastings?

Psst! Mademoiselle! May I have a little word with you?

If you wish, Monsieur Poirot.

You know that Monsieur Giraud suspects your friend, Jack Renauld?

Perhaps he does ... but I know Jack is innocent! I must tell you something Monsieur Giraud doesn't know.

A few hours before he died, I saw Monsieur Renauld. He was arguing with a stranger!

Let us go and find out what Jack was doing at the Villa that night ...

Jack Renauld is under arrest for his father's murder! Please accompany me to the library, and I'll explain everything.

The dispute between the two men gave us the motive. As to the means, Jack was in Merlinville that night. Then we found a second victim, stabbed with the same dagger. Only Jack could have taken it ...

You are wrong! Somebody else could have taken it.

Allow me to continue. Jack slipped into the greenhouse and killed his accomplice. And Madame Renauld lied to protect the murderer. For who else would she lie?

There is one thing you have failed to take into account. If Jack believed he was to inherit, why would he bury his father's body? It was in his interest that it be discovered quickly!

Poirot, there is someone we have overlooked — Georges Conneau, Madame Beroldy's lover.

Yes, like you I believe Conneau is still alive, or *was* until recently.

Let us suppose that after his escape he became a ruthless criminal. He comes to Merlinville, where he happens to find the woman he never ceased to love ...

She is living under an assumed name with a rich Englishman. The two meet and quarrel, and Conneau stabs Renauld. At that moment, Madame Daubreuil appears. The murderer drags her into the greenhouse before falling down in an epileptic fit ...

Now suppose that Jack Renauld comes on the scene. Madame Daubreuil tells him about her past and warns of the danger to her daughter. They make a pact and Jack convinces his mother to become an accomplice. She permits herself to be gagged and bound ...

You should write for the cinema, *mon ami!* But *my* theory happens to be the truth. Remember how Monsieur Renauld changed after he came to Merlinville? Consider also his friendship with Madame Daubreuil, and the large sums of money paid to her. Then Monsieur Renauld quarrelled with Jack over his son's wish to marry Marthe Daubreuil. The next day Renauld altered his will, leaving his fortune to his wife.

Ten days later he wrote to me, imploring my assistance.

Renauld sent his son a cable, bidding him leave for Argentina ... That evening he was visited by a mysterious lady.

Does that shed new light on the matter, *mon ami*?

You mean Georges Conneau was blackmailing him?

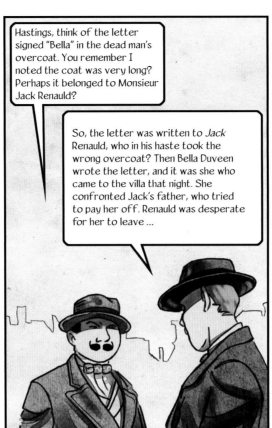

Hastings, think of the letter signed "Bella" in the dead man's overcoat. You remember I noted the coat was very long? Perhaps it belonged to Monsieur Jack Renauld?

So, the letter was written to *Jack* Renauld, who in his haste took the wrong overcoat? Then Bella Duveen wrote the letter, and it was she who came to the villa that night. She confronted Jack's father, who tried to pay her off. Renauld was desperate for her to leave ...

But why, Poirot?

For one very simple reason. Monsieur Renauld had arranged for a murder to take place that night.

But what about the second victim? Did you not say it was Conneau, the lover of Renauld's wife?

But, *mon ami*, do you not understand me? Conneau and Renauld are one and the same!

We know how dearly Madame Renauld loved her husband. Now, did Madame Dubreuil not blackmail Renauld? And is it not a fact that we know nothing of Renauld's past? He could not allow his son to marry the daughter of his former accomplice. There was only one way out.

He planned his own death?

Yes, Hastings. But he did not intend to die. He would flee to another country, to be joined in time by his wife. All they needed was a body to substitute for him ...

And fortuitously, a vagabond comes into the garden one day. He and Renauld fight, the tramp suffers an epileptic fit, and dies!

So Renauld and his wife quickly conceive a plan. Nobody from the house must see the body. Madame Renauld alone must identify it.

Renauld sent me a letter asking for help, in order to impress the magistrate. The paper-knife was used a murder weapon, to give Madame Renauld's story credence. She was bound and gagged by her husband, who left through the window, smoothing his footprints as he left. He went to the golf course and, having used a lead pipe to disfigure the victim's face, began to dig a grave ...

And then?

Then he was stabbed in the back! The cunning murderer availed himself of the same devices used by Renauld. This has been a particularly perplexing mystery.

You're marvellous, Poirot, absolutely marvellous!

Whereas Giraud found one clue and followed the wrong trail! No method, Hastings!

Poor Madame Renauld. To find that it was her husband who had been murdered. And then to find her son accused ...

And forced to admit that Madame Daubreuil was her husband's mistress, rather than admit the truth of the blackmail.

And the dagger, Poirot? There must have been two of them?

Certainly! They were duplicates, and one belongs to Jack. But far more significant is the question of Jack's heredity. As the saying has it ...

Like father, like son!

You mean Jack, as George Conneau's son, is capable of anything?

Exactly! *Mon ami*, what time is the afternoon boat for England from Calais?

About five o'clock, I believe.

We shall just have time to catch it!

LATER ON ...

Are you going to explain why we are here, Poirot?

We are going to look for a witness, *mon cher* Hastings — Miss Bella Duveen ... I know nothing about her, but I can guess a good deal. She is sure to be on stage, and it is likely she should be the first love of Jack Renauld, a young man with plenty of money. I found this photograph among Monsieur Jack's belongings.

Good heavens, it's Cinderella! Surely she can't be involved in this dreadful business!

What's the matter, *mon ami?* Are you feeling seasick?

As soon as we reach London, we must visit an acquaintance of mine, a theatrical agent.

Bella Duveen? I know the name ...

By the Lord! It's the Dulcibella Kids! They're sisters — acrobats, dancers. They're appearing tonight at the Coventry Theatre.

"And now, ladies and gentlemen, the Dulcibella Kids!"

Haven't we seen enough, Poirot? I must get some air ...

Go, by all means, *mon ami*. But I am enjoying myself!

LATER, AT A HOTEL NEAR THE THEATRE ...

Good heavens! Cinderella!

I saw you sitting at the front ... you and your friend. He's the famous detective, isn't he?

Er ... yes.

Don't cry, child. You're safe here. I'll take care of you. I know everything ...

Oh, but you don't!

It was you who took the dagger, wasn't it?

Yes.

But why?

I was afraid there would be fingerprints on it. Are you going to give me up to the police?

No, Cinderella, I won't. Because I love you.

You came to see Mr Renauld that night. He tried to give you money, but you refused it. You left, but waited outside ...

You saw a man leave, wearing Jack's overcoat. You'd threatened to kill him before, in your letter. Your anger drove you mad, and you struck.

You're right, you're right! And you still love me?

I cannot help myself Cinderella. Love has been too strong for me.

?

Oh, no! No!

Hastings. Let her go. I shall not pursue her.

Love has changed you, Hastings. Why did you not tell me you knew this girl?

Poirot, I'm sorry. But sometimes one has no choice. And I'm certain Miss Duveen was not involved in the crime. I travelled home from France with her that day, and I would swear to that in a court of law!

41

THE NEXT DAY.

So you are my enemy now, Hastings... But does your blind faith in Miss Duveen prevent you from realizing that Jack Renauld may now be wrongly convicted? That would be your fault.

We must pay a visit to Monsieur Hautet. I wish to know how Jack Renauld intends to conduct his defence.

I was told you had returned to England, Monsieur Poirot. I am glad to see that is not the case. Frankly, many points are still obscure to me.

Will you permit me to be present during Jack Renauld's interrogation? I have some sympathy for the boy.

I have a letter for you, Poirot.

Many thanks, I shall return this evidence to you tomorrow.

You've come to observe the conclusion of the case? Jack Renauld is making no attempt to defend himself. It's extraordinary!

Indeed. It gives one pause to think, *eh*, Giraud?

I'm glad you're satisfied of young Renauld's guilt at last.

But I am not in the least satisfied! Jack Renauld is innocent.

That infernal Giraud will pay for his crowing!

Why, Stonor! What are you doing here?

I must stand by Jack Renauld. I'll never believe he is a murderer. But can it be proved?

He's behaving very queerly, Poirot. I implore you, save him!

That may be difficult ...

THE NEXT DAY, BEFORE THE MAGISTRATE ...

Monsieur Renauld, do you recognize this weapon?

Yes, it's a war souvenir, which I gave to my mother as a present.

Jack is heading for disaster ... Look!

Are you Mr Hautet, the examining magistrate?

?!

Yes, madame, but I forbid —

Poirot! That's not Cinderella! Could it be her sister?

My name is Bella Duveen!

"Bella was so in love with Jack! She got it into her head that he was keen on another girl and she made up her mind to go to Merlinville and try to see him. I tried everything to stop her from going."

"My dear Hastings — By the time you read this letter Bella will have given herself up. I'm tired out with struggling. However, I owe you an explanation ..."

"The next day Bella ha arranged to meet me the hotel, but she ne turned up. Then I rea about that awful crim in the paper."

"I decided to go to the villa, where I ran up against you. Then I saw the dead man ..."

"There was only one thing for me to do: get hold of the dagger and escape with it. I pretended to faint ..."

"I took the train for Calais and then the boat to England. When we were in mid-Channel I threw the dagger into the sea."

"Bella was already in London, looking like nothing on earth. I told her what I'd done and she began laughing ... it was horrible. But we had to continue our tour. And then I saw you in Coventry that night ... That's all I can say."

It's signed "Cinder — Dulcie Duveen".

44

Did you know all the time that it was the sister?

Yes, *mon ami*. But I said nothing to you because I was hurt at your lack of faith in me.

She doesn't say whether or not she cares for me ...

VILLA GENEVIÈVE, AT NIGHTFALL ...

Poirot, are you going to tell me what we're doing?

Keep quiet. We have set a trap!

Help! Help!

Marthe Daubreuil!

45

Yes! Young Marthe Dubreuil was the killer of Monsieur Renauld, and I knew she would return to murder Madame Renauld as well. I needed someone to prevent it — and *voilà*, I called upon the acrobatic prowess of Mademoiselle Dulcie Duveen!

Marthe Dubreuil's mother had extracted thousands from Monsieur Renauld. She was, after all, the notorious Jeanne Beroldy, and her daughter was just as greedy! Marthe knew that Monsieur Renauld opposed her marrying Jack, so she decided to kill him. Jack had already given her the third dagger, identical to the others.

Once Renauld was dead, Marthe knew she could marry Jack. He was heir to a fortune! But she would need to kill Madame Renauld as well for them to inherit it all.

Dulcie Duveen suspected her sister had killed Monsieur Renauld as an act of revenge because she thought the dagger was Bella's. So she stole it and threw it into the sea. I realized then that the murder weapon must have been the one belonging to Marthe Daubreuil!

A happy ending! Cinderella prevented the death of Madame Renauld — and found Prince Charming, *eh*, Hastings?!

THE END